KIDS GET CODING

STAYING SAFE ONLINE

Heather Lyons & Elizabeth Tweedale

Contents

Getting started

Hi! I'm Data Duck! I'm going to help you learn all about how to use the Internet safely as you travel through the digital world.

In order to be crafty coders in the future, we need to learn how to be **Internet Superheroes** who explore lots of incredible places online and keep our private information safe and away from strangers.

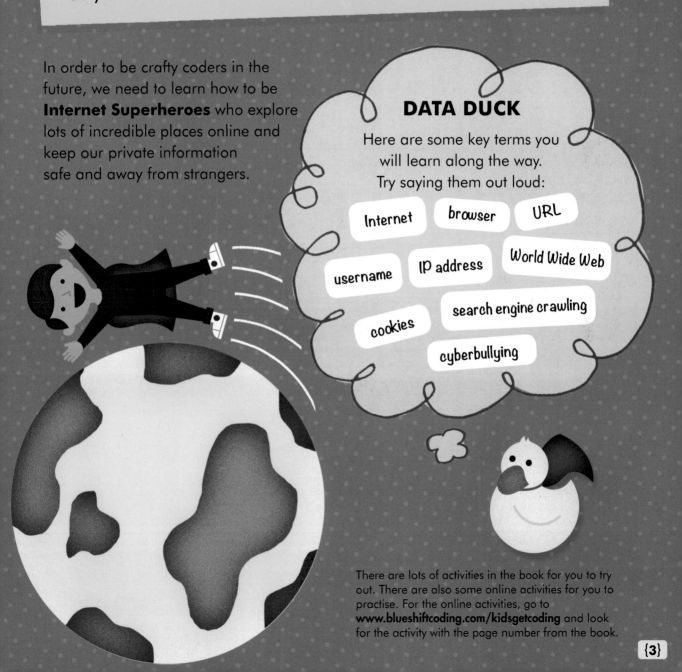

DATA DUCK

Here are some key terms you will learn along the way. Try saying them out loud:

Internet   browser   URL

username   IP address   World Wide Web

cookies   search engine crawling

cyberbullying

There are lots of activities in the book for you to try out. There are also some online activities for you to practise. For the online activities, go to **www.blueshiftcoding.com/kidsgetcoding** and look for the activity with the page number from the book.

What is the Internet?

The Internet is a gigantic network of computers that are all connected together. It lives on digital devices around the world.

These computers can be very big and powerful, or much smaller like a phone. Computers connected to the Internet use it to send little packages of information (called 'data') to one another. We can think of it like a very, very fast postal service!

DATA DUCK

We can view some of the information on the Internet as web pages. These web pages make up the World Wide Web.

Internet city

The way the Internet and World Wide Web work together is like a city. The roads are the Internet cables connecting everything together. The buildings are all the computers, big and small. The vehicles that travel on the roads, such as cars, are the information (web pages) moving around. Let's have a go at creating our own Internet city!

Instructions:
1. Draw a road network on some paper.
2. Add some buildings.
3. Draw a truck.
4. Draw a car.
5. Draw a motorcycle.
6. Draw a bicycle.

Use different colours to help you understand your Internet city: green for what represents Internet cables, red for what represents computers and blue for what represents web pages.

Browsing the Web

To find what you are looking for on the World Wide Web, you need to use a special program on your computer or phone called a web browser.

Some popular web browsers are Chrome, Safari, Firefox, Internet Explorer and Opera. A browser can find and show content on the World Wide Web, including web pages, images and videos.

All the web pages on the Internet have a specific address, which is how we find them. This is known as a URL (or Uniform Resource Locator). The address for google is www.google.com.

URLs get more complicated when we go beyond the home page of a website.

When we type each part of the URL into an address bar, we are helping to direct the browser to a specific web page.

https://www.hachettechildrens.co.uk/books/detail.page?isbn=9780750297028

The name of the way web pages are sent to your computer. The 's' at the end means it has been sent securely

World Wide Web

Company, school or organisation

Extension showing the home country or type of organisation

Section of the website the page is stored in

The specific web page – the '?' means it has come from a database

Build a URL

Imagine you are building a web page for yourself on the blueshift website. On a piece of paper, can you put the blocks below into the right order to make a correct URL?

Try typing this address into your browser. What do you find?

Turn to page 23 to see the answers.

#activity.html

www.

http://

kidsgetcoding/

blueshiftcoding.

internetsafety/

com/

DATA DUCK

We are 'online' when we are connected to the Internet. Our computer, phone or tablet needs some sort of connection to see pages through a web browser.

These are some of the pictures that your computer or phone might display if it is online:

(4G)

Search engines

Because there is so much 'stuff' on the Internet, we often need help finding things. A search engine helps us to find web pages that contain the information we need.

A search engine, like Google, uses a sort of robot called a 'crawler' to go through all the web pages on the Internet. The crawler looks at the content and keeps a record of all the words it finds.

These words are then sorted and organised into an 'index', which is like an enormous catalogue. When we search for something using the search engine, it will use the index to create a list of results for us.

DATA DUCK
There are over a TRILLION individual pages on the Web and that number is growing every day!

Higher or lower

A search engine uses certain steps to sort through information, just like a computer programmer uses an algorithm when they're writing code.

Let's imagine some of the steps a search engine might use to find information in an index. Ask someone to think of a number from one to eight. Follow the questions below to find their number in three guesses or less!

Can you see a pattern in the way the questions are asked?

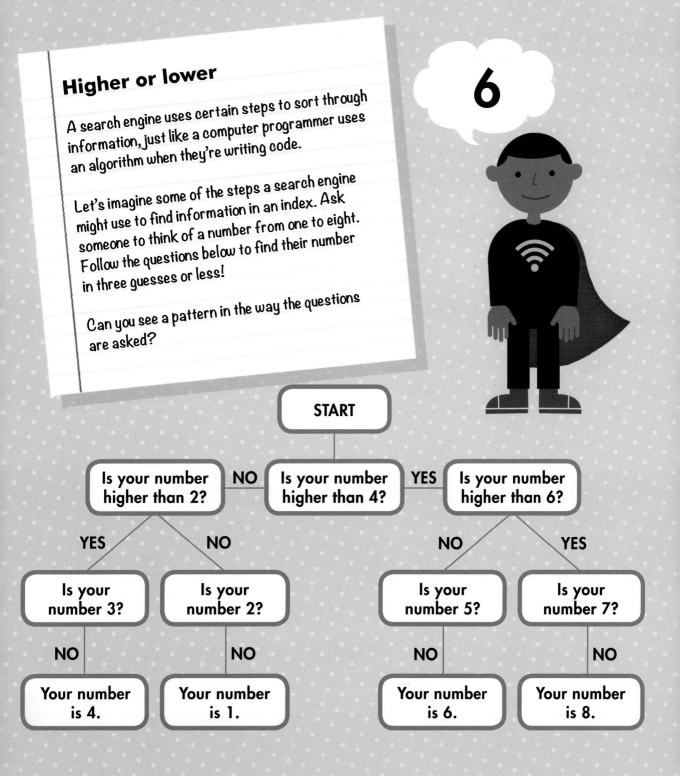

START

Is your number higher than 2? **NO** Is your number higher than 4? **YES** Is your number higher than 6?

YES **NO**

Is your number 3? Is your number 2?

NO **YES**

Is your number 5? Is your number 7?

NO

Your number is 4.

NO

Your number is 1.

NO

Your number is 6.

NO

Your number is 8.

Cookies!

Web pages use 'cookies' to keep track of us online. Every time we visit a web page, a cookie stores this information, and it begins to build up a picture of our online behaviour.

A cookie is a little piece of information that a website sends to our computers. It then sends back information to the website about us, such as the things we click on and how much time is spent on the website.

Cookies can sometimes make it easier for us to use a website. For example, if we are shopping, cookies will help the website to provide information about things we might like to buy.

DATA DUCK

The first time we visit a website, a cookie is downloaded on to our computer browser that records how we used the site. The next time we visit that website, our browser checks to see if it has a cookie from that site already. If it does, the browser sends the cookie back to the website to help it remember us, and to be updated with new information.

Cookie trail

It's important to remember that cookies keep track of what you do online.

Hansel is dropping bits of chocolate chip cookies at some sites. Gretel is dropping bits of peanut butter sandwich at other sites.

Which sites do they both like? Which sites does only Gretel visit?

Turn to page 23 to see the answers.

CBBC

KidsReads

Pottermore

NASA Kids' Club

Art Games

Club Penguin

Going places

We can use the Internet to visit lots of websites online. We can do our shopping, get directions to a museum or watch a football match.

The web pages we can look at online come from all around the world and are created by many different computer programmers. This means we have to stay safe online, just as we do in the 'real world'.

In the real world, we wouldn't go to places we are unsure about and we wouldn't give strangers our name and address.

It's important to always tell a grown up you trust if you see something online that you're unsure about. It is also a good idea to use your computer when a grown up is nearby, so that you can ask them questions easily about the things you do online.

All computers and other digital devices that are connected to the Internet have their own address called an IP (Internet Protocol) address. An IP address has four groups of numbers and looks something like this: 10.98.242.173.

What would you do ...

- if you saw something online that made you upset or uncomfortable?

- if you were online and a strange, flashing window popped up asking you to click on it?

- if you were on a web page and it asked you for your name?

- if someone said something mean about a picture you put online?

Turn to page 23 to see the answers.

DATA DUCK

IP addresses show people the country and city your device is in, and the way you are accessing the Internet. You can discover your IP address by typing 'IP address' into Google.

130.26.153.33

Keep it private

Sometimes we go to websites and we are asked to give information about ourselves.

Websites are usually built by people we don't know, and it's these people who are asking us questions. It's important not to reveal private information to strangers.

If you are ever unsure about which information you should give out online, just ask yourself if you would give it to a stranger in the real world.

Being an Internet superhero means staying safe and being smart online. Don't forget, most superheroes wear masks to keep their identity a secret!

DATA DUCK

Remember, when we put information into a website, people we do not know can see our answers.

Be a real Internet superhero!

Below is a form from a shopping website online. To be an Internet Superhero you should only fill out the parts that keep your secret identity safe!

On a piece of paper, write down which pieces of information you think you should give.

Turn to page 23 to see the answers.

SHOP ONLINE   Toys   Games   Books   **My Basket**

Your name	
Your school's name	
Your pet's name	
Your parents' names	
Your birthday	
Your favourite colour	
Your parents' email address	
Your favourite sports team	
A picture of you	
Your parents' phone number	
Your address	

Our digital identity

Our digital identity is all the information about us that is on the Web. It is made up of everything that we put online.

Every time we post a photo or video, or write something, it makes up part of our digital identity. Once it is stored somewhere on the Internet, it may not ever be possible to delete it.

DATA DUCK
All the data we put online about ourselves is like a tattoo. It is a permanent collection of information about us, available online for others to find.

Lisa Smith 7th April

8

My mum baked me an amazing cake for my birthday today!

So far we've learnt about three ways information about us can get stored online:

- Cookies
- IP addresses
- Information you put into forms on web pages

What do you think the cookies, IP addresses and forms you have used say about you?

Even when we are careful not to put too much personal information on one website, if we post different things across lots of websites someone can still gather that information together to find out who we are.

Putting clues together

Dotted around these two pages are things posted by somebody on different websites. Write a paragraph about what you have learnt about them from the information they have posted. Can you see how easy it is to form a picture of someone's life by what they leave online?

LisaMovieQueen:
Funny films are my favourite. This was SO good, and the main character looks just like me!

Amazing goal by Freddy Footwork

LisaMovieQueen:
What a great game! I'm so lucky that Birmingham United are my home team.

Super security!

The Internet wouldn't be any fun if we had to keep everything private. The best thing about the Internet is that it allows us to share information with our friends and see really exciting stuff.

When we post things like our work or pictures of ourselves on a website, we should ask ourselves some questions:

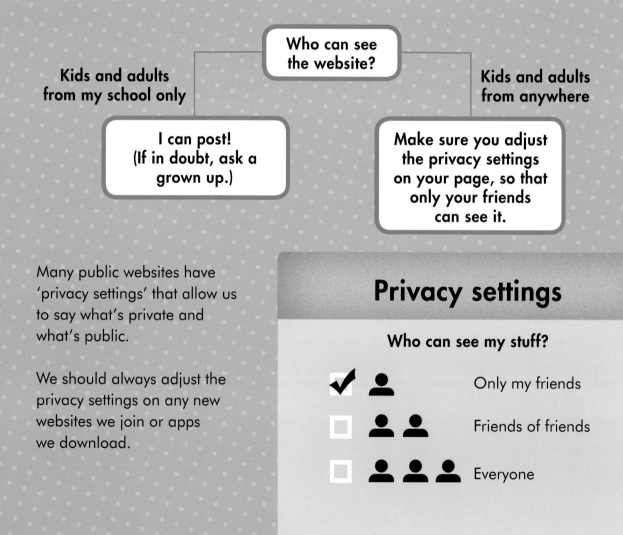

Who can see the website?

Kids and adults from my school only

Kids and adults from anywhere

I can post!
(If in doubt, ask a grown up.)

Make sure you adjust the privacy settings on your page, so that only your friends can see it.

Many public websites have 'privacy settings' that allow us to say what's private and what's public.

We should always adjust the privacy settings on any new websites we join or apps we download.

Privacy settings

Who can see my stuff?

✔ 👤 Only my friends

☐ 👤👤 Friends of friends

☐ 👤👤👤 Everyone

Websites will often ask us if we have an account and to 'log in'. This means that we need a username and password to access the site's main information.

It is important that we make up usernames and passwords that we can remember. Don't use the same ones every time and never give away a superhero password. It's a secret!

My secret names and passwords

Can you think of some good usernames? Write down five on a piece of paper.

What secret passwords can you think of? Make sure they can't be guessed! Try to use letters and numbers in your password. Write down your top five!

Top secret

Top secret

For some help making secret passwords go to: **www.blueshiftcoding.com/kidsgetcoding** for our top secret password creator.

Sharing is caring

There are lots of websites that kids and adults use to share information with each other. These sorts of websites are called 'social media' websites.

A social media website is one where we have an account and we can share information about ourselves. Some of these websites are Facebook, Twitter and Instagram.

Most social media websites are only for people who are 13 and over. Many websites will ask us for our birthday before we sign up to them, to make sure that we do not see things that are not meant for kids.

DATA DUCK
We can connect with friends and strangers on social media websites. This means we should be very careful about who we make our 'friend' on a social media site and whether we know and can trust them. Sometimes baddies are hiding their real identity and aren't actually who they say they are!

Sometimes, people say mean things online. This is called 'cyberbullying'. When we see something online that worries us, we should always tell a grown up.

Internet superheroes know that they shouldn't say things to people online if they wouldn't say them in person.

Careful commenting

Data Duck posted a picture on his school website and lots of his classmates commented back. Here are some of the things that people wrote:

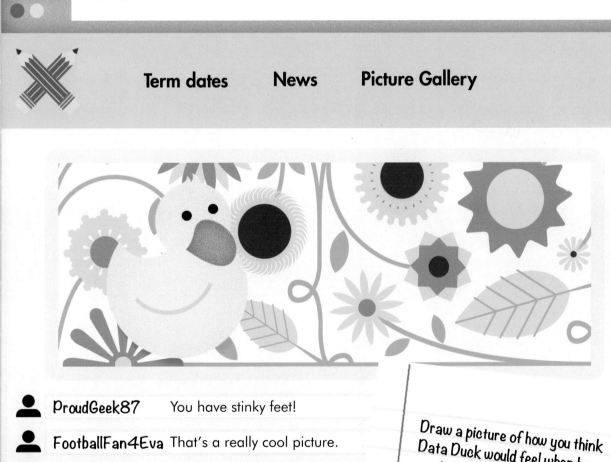

Term dates   **News**   **Picture Gallery**

👤 ProudGeek87   You have stinky feet!

👤 FootballFan4Eva That's a really cool picture.

👤 BookLover12   I like how you drew the flower.

👤 TimeToShine   You are my best friend.

Draw a picture of how you think Data Duck would feel when he read these comments.

Top tips

In this book, you've learned about many things you need to do to become an Internet Superhero and stay safe online. Let's have a recap:

- Many of the websites on the Internet are run by strangers, so when you add private information to websites, you are giving that information to a stranger.
- If in doubt, do not give away your name, age, school, birth date or where you live to anyone online.
- Do not trust everyone online. People are not always who they say they are.
- If you see or read something online that bothers you, tell a grown up!
- Always use the Internet with a grown up nearby.
- Remember to keep your identity secret at all times.

Words to remember

browser	the program we use to access the World Wide Web.
cookies	packets of information that keep track of your online behaviour.
cyberbullying	bullying that happens on the Internet.
Internet	a giant network of computers that are all connected together.
IP address	four groups of numbers that make up an address that identifies a computer or digital device connected to the Internet.
search engine crawling	when robots called crawlers travel from web page to web page, keeping track of the information they find.
URL	the address of a specific website.
username	the name you are known by on a website where you have an account.

Activity answers

Page 7

http://www.blueshiftcoding.com/kidsgetcoding/
internetsafety/#activity.html

Page 11

Both Hansel and Gretel visit NASA Kids' Club.
Only Gretel visits Pottermore and Club Penguin.

Page 13

1. If you see something online that makes you
upset or unsure, you should talk to a grown up
you trust.

2. If a strange flashing window appears on
your screen, you should tell a grown up. Some
content that is sent through the Internet is not
appropriate for children and may contain
nasty messages!

3. If in doubt, do not give your name to
anyone online.

4. If someone says something mean about a
picture you post online, you should tell a grown
up. Cyberbullying is never okay.

Page 15

It's safe to give out your favourite colour or your
sports team. It may be okay to give out your
pet's name, as long as you don't give away any
other information about where you live or parks
you play in. You shouldn't give out anything
else. Remember, the more pieces of information
you give, the more strangers can form a picture
of who you are.

Index

Published in paperback in 2017 by Wayland

Copyright © Hodder & Stoughton, 2017

All rights reserved.

Editors: Annabel Stones and Liza Miller
Illustration: Alex Westgate
Freelance editor: Katie Woolley
Designer: Anthony Hannant (LittleRedAnt)

ISBN: 9780750297516
10 9 8 7 6 5 4 3 2 1

MIX
Paper from
responsible sources
FSC® C104740

Wayland
An imprint of
Hachette Children's Group
Part of Hodder & Stoughton
Carmelite House
50 Victoria Embankment
London EC4Y 0DZ

An Hachette UK Company
www.hachette.co.uk
www.hachettechildrens.co.uk

Printed in China